B IS FOR BIBLE

a coloring book for kids

B IS FOR BIBLE

In the beginning God
created the heavens
and the earth.

God created Adam as the
first human.
Then He created a woman for
Adam from Adam's rib.
She was named Eve.

And the Lord God formed man
of the dust of
the ground, and breathed into
his nostrils the
breath of life; and man became
a living soul.
Genesis 2:7 KJV

1 JOHN 4:19
WE LOVE BECAUSE HE FIRST LOVED US.

BE QUICK TO LISTEN

Be SLOW to speak or get angry. James 1:19

Joshua 1:9
"Have I not commanded you? Be strong and courageous.
Do not be frightened, and do not be dismayed, for the
LORD your God is with you wherever you go."

Ephesians 4:32

"Be kind to one another, tenderhearted, forgiving one another, as God in Christ forgave you."

Galatians 5:22-23
But the fruit of the Spirit is love, joy, peace, patience, kindness, goodness, faithfulness, gentleness, and self-control.

Let your
LIGHT SHINE

Matthew 5:16

1 Chronicles 16:34:
Give thanks to the Lord for He is good; His love endures forever.

NUMBERS 6:24

THE LORD BLESS YOU AND KEEP YOU.

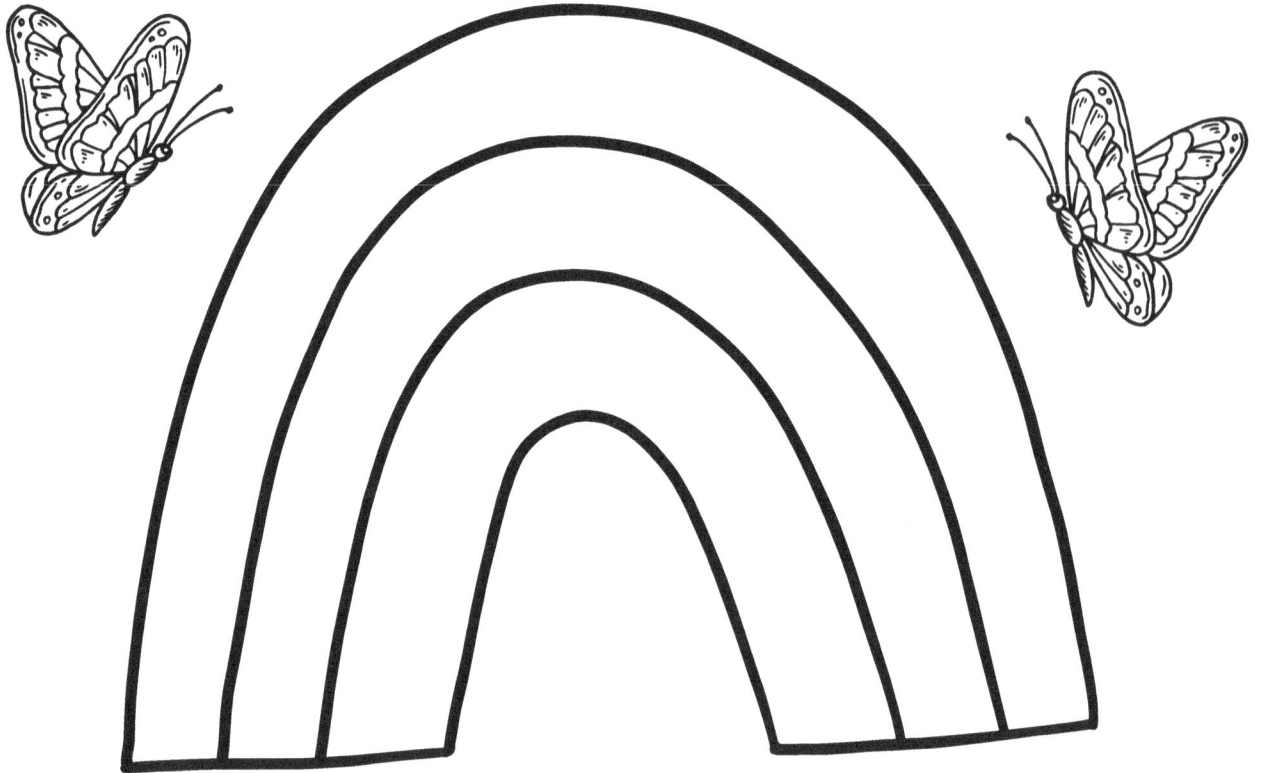

1 Timothy 4:12

Don't let anyone look down on you because you are young, but set an example for the believers in speech, in conduct, in love, in faith and in purity.

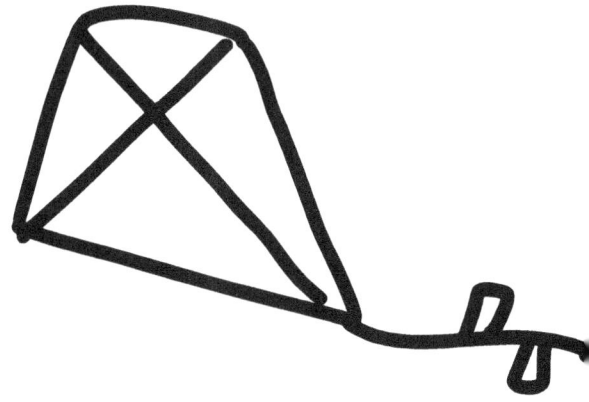

PSALMS 56:3

WHEN I'M AFRAID, I PUT MY TRUST IN YOU!

Psalm 119:105:
Your word is a lamp for my feet, a light on my path.

John 10:11:
I am the good shepherd.
The good shepherd lays
down his life for the sheep.

Matthew 22:39
"And a second is like it: You shall love your neighbor as yourself."

HEBREWS 13:8 JESUS CHRIST IS THE SAME YESTERDAY, TODAY, AND FOREVER.

Philippians 4:4
"Rejoice in the Lord always; again I will say, rejoice!"

Isaiah 30:15

"For thus said the Lord GOD, the Holy One of Israel, 'In returning and rest you shall be saved; in quietness and in trust shall be your strength."

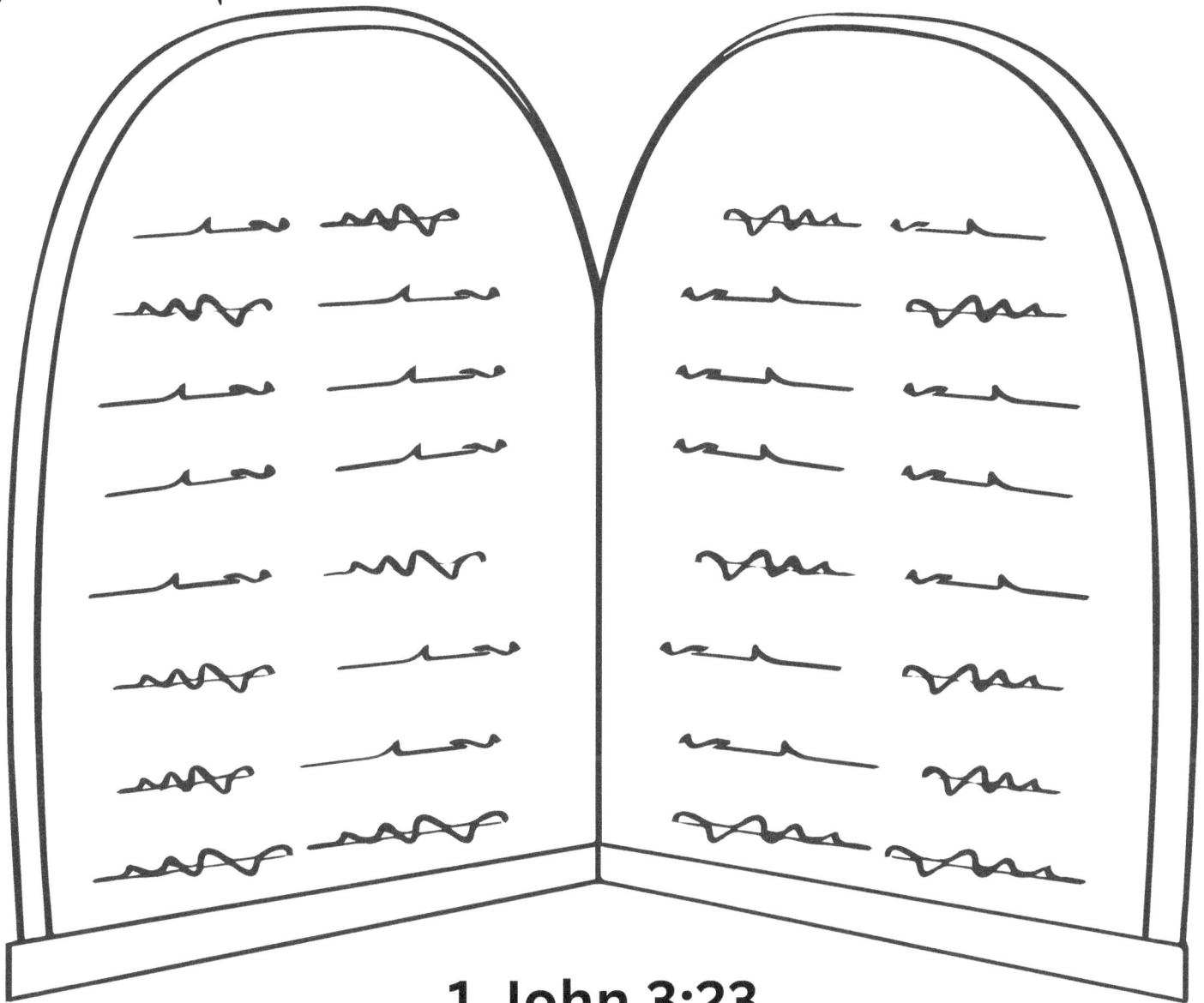

1 John 3:23

"And this is his commandment, that
we believe in the name of his Son
Jesus Christ and love one another,
just as he has commanded us."

PSALM 145:9

"THE LORD IS GOOD TO ALL, AND HIS MERCY IS OVER ALL THAT HE HAS MADE."

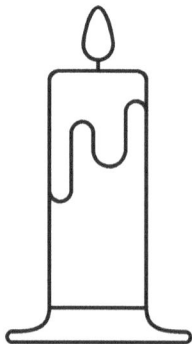

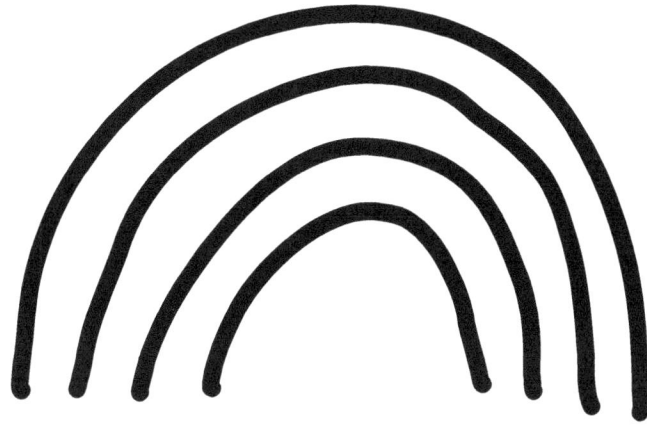

. Psalm 56:3
"When I am afraid, I put
my trust in you."

Psalm 119:105
"Your word is a lamp
to my feet and a light
to my path."

Psalms 96

Sing to the LORD

The **LORD**

gives wisdom

Proverbs 2:6

Jesus said
I AM
the
LIGHT
of the
WORLD

John 8:12

COLOSSIANS 3:20

"CHILDREN, OBEY YOUR PARENTS IN EVERYTHING, FOR THIS PLEASES THE LORD."

Romans 3:23
"For all have sinned
and fall short of
the glory of God."

Psalm 118:24

"This is the day that the LORD has made; let us rejoice and be glad in it."

Romans 10:13
"For everyone who calls on the name of the Lord will be saved."

Matthew 5:14
"You are the light of the
world. A city set on a hill
cannot be hidden."

PROVERBS 3:5 "TRUST IN THE LORD WITH ALL YOUR HEART, AND DO NOT LEAN ON YOUR OWN UNDERSTANDING."